# THE SECRETS & LIES OF MILITARY WIVES

**Title:** *The Secrets and Lies of Military Wives*
**Author:** Jenna Lumb

**Copyright © 2025 by Jenna Lumb**
All rights reserved. No part of this book may be copied, reproduced, stored, or transmitted in any form or by any means—electronic, mechanical, photocopying, recording, or otherwise—without prior written permission from the author, except for brief excerpts used in reviews, articles, or educational purposes.

This is a work of nonfiction inspired by real events. However, names, characters, and identifying details have been altered or fictionalized to protect the privacy of individuals. Any resemblance to actual persons, living or deceased, is purely coincidental.

Published by: Self-published on Amazon KDP

**Cover Design by:** Jenna Lumb
**Illustrations by:** Jenna Lumb

For inquiries, permissions, or licensing, please contact:
Lumbjenna@gmail.com

# Acknowledgments

Writing this book has been a wild ride—equal parts therapy session, gossip hour, and an inside joke that got way out of hand. But I couldn't have done it alone.

First and foremost, to my husband—the real MVP, the reason I know firsthand how ridiculous (and wonderful) military life can be. Thank you for loving me through my wild ideas, my late-night writing binges, and my endless need to document the drama that finds me. You are my rock, my partner-in-crime, and the one who puts up with my nonsense without (too much) complaint.

To my amazing daughter, who reminds me every day that the world is full of curiosity, joy, and new stories waiting to be told. I hope you always stay unapologetically yourself.

To my family and friends—especially those who have shared their stories, laughed at my jokes, and assured me that, no, I'm not insane for writing this book—your support means the world.

To every military spouse who has ever rolled their eyes at a Dependapotamus, survived a PCS move with their sanity intact, or debated committing a small crime while dealing with Tricare—this one's for you.

To my readers, the ones who stayed up way too late with this book, nodding along and thinking, *Yep, I know someone exactly like that*—thank you. You get it. And I appreciate you more than you know.

And finally, to Murphy's Law, for never failing to prove that if it can go wrong, it will. You may be an absolute menace, but at least you made for some good stories. Here's to the chaos, the secrets, the lies, and most importantly—the tea.

# Introduction

Hi there. Hello. Welcome. Go ahead—grab a drink, sit down, get cozy. You're going to want to be comfortable for this. I've got stories to tell. Think of me as your narrator, the fly on the wall of this drama-filled circus we call military life. You don't know me yet, but by the end of this, you might feel like we've been friends for years, swapping secrets over coffee—or tequila. Dealer's choice.

Here's the thing: I'm here to spill the tea. No sugar-coating, no filters, just real stories about real people, with enough chaos to make you wonder how any of us manage to function. This isn't one of those sanitized, Instagram-perfect depictions of military life. Nope. This is the real stuff, the kind of messy truth that keeps it interesting.

Military life? It's basically a zoo. You've got all kinds of characters here. There are the girl bosses who juggle three jobs, two kids, and a perfectly staged Instagram feed that somehow doesn't include the dirty dishes in their sink. Then there are the trashy spouses—the ones who smell like weed and insist it's "for medical purposes," even though you've seen them try to hotbox the base housing laundry room. You've got the racists (yes, we see you), the cheaters turning FRG meetings into reality TV episodes, the abusers who hide behind perfect family photos, and the ones who somehow wind up on the evening news. Every base has a little of everything.

I've seen it all. I've heard it all. And now, you're about to read it all.

Oh, but here's the twist: I'm not just some disembodied narrator telling you about other people's chaos. My story? It's right here too, hidden between the lines. Somewhere in this tangled web of drama, you'll find me—just another military spouse, doing my best to survive the circus. Think you can figure out who I am? Good luck. I'm not making it easy for you.

So buckle up. This ride's about to get wild, and there's no seatbelt big enough for the kind of drama you're about to dive into. These stories? They're raw, they're real, and they're everything you didn't know you needed. Let's get started.

# Peppermint Tea

Alright, buckle up, because we're diving headfirst into the wonderful, confusing, and slightly ridiculous world of military acronyms. If you thought texting abbreviations like "LOL" and "BRB" were annoying, you ain't seen nothing yet. The military doesn't just use acronyms; they breathe them. They live them. They weaponize them. And if you're a spouse, you're stuck in the splash zone.

Let's start with the basics:

PCS – Permanent Change of Station.

Spoiler alert: there's nothing "permanent" about it. PCS is the government's way of saying, "Pack up your entire life and move across the country, or the globe, with two months' notice." And don't forget the added bonus of housing waitlists, broken furniture, and finding out your new base's idea of "luxury living" includes black mold and a busted HVAC.

POA – Power of Attorney.

This is the golden ticket that lets you sign your spouse's name on everything while they're deployed. Car registration? Yep. Housing paperwork? Sure. Selling their Xbox on Craigslist because they pissed you off before they left? Technically, yes—but you didn't hear that from me.

DFAC – Dining Facility.

Where dreams (and taste buds) go to die. Unless you're stationed somewhere fancy like Germany or Korea, you'll quickly learn that "free food" isn't always worth it. Bonus points if you can pronounce what they're serving.

FTS – Full-Time Support.

Not to be confused with what you wish your partner would give you during deployment.

NJP – Non-Judicial Punishment.

Also known as "your husband did something stupid, and now you have to deal with the consequences." This is the military equivalent of being grounded but way less fun. If you hear "NJP" at the FRG meeting, sit down and pour some tea.

FRG – Family Readiness Group.

Ah, the FRG—the place where spouses come together to support each other, swap info, and (let's be real) spread gossip faster than a wildfire on a windy day. You think you're there to hear about deployment updates, but you're really there to find out who's getting divorced, who's cheating, and who's on the verge of an NJP.

UA – Unauthorized Absence.

For civilians, this is "playing hooky." For service members, it's a career-ending mistake. For spouses? It's the drama you live for.

OPSEC – Operational Security.

Translation: don't tell Karen from high school your husband's deployment schedule. In fact, don't even tell your mom. The military is big on keeping things hush-hush, and trust me, you don't want to be "that spouse" who spills classified info on Facebook.

TAD/TDY – Temporary Assigned Duty/Temporary Duty.

This is when your spouse disappears for a few weeks or months, and you suddenly have the whole bed to yourself. Sure, it sounds lonely, but you'll learn to enjoy the small victories—like eating cereal for dinner and not hearing "what's for dinner?" 500 times a day.

BOHICA – Bend Over, Here It Comes Again.

Not an official acronym, but if you've ever dealt with Tricare, housing, or any part of the military system, you know this one's accurate.

MILSO – Military Significant Other.

You. Congrats! You're now part of the MILSO club, which comes with a lifetime supply of sleepless nights, acronyms you don't understand, and figuring out how to explain to people why your spouse calls it a "cover" instead of a hat.

SNAFU/FUBAR – Situation Normal, All Fucked Up / Fucked Up Beyond All Recognition.

Used to describe everything from your spouse's schedule to your PCS move to the entire military system on a good day.

And last but not least…

HUA – Heard, Understood, Acknowledged.

This is what your spouse says when their boss gives them an order, and it's also what you should say the next time they try to explain something that sounds like alien code.

Now, dear reader, you might be thinking, "Why do I need to know all this? I'm just here to survive the next deployment." And you'd be right! But trust me, there's nothing quite as satisfying as throwing out an acronym mid-conversation and watching your spouse do a double take.

So study up, take notes, and remember: when in doubt, just nod and say "HUA." You'll fit right in.

# Trish

Our first story starts in Base housing. Where the walls are thin, the drama is thick, and no secret stays hidden for long. It was 2006, in a cozy little cul-de-sac, where two families lived side by side in their cookie-cutter duplexes. On the left, we had Rachel, her three kids, and her husband, Mark, the easygoing type who always offered to mow the neighbor's lawn. On the right was Trish, her four kids, and her husband, Ben, who was currently deployed. And yes, that's where the chaos begins.

The trouble started innocently enough. One sunny afternoon, Mark's best friend, the guy we'll call Danny, showed up with a couple of duffle bags and a sheepish grin. "Just a few weeks," he said, parking himself on Rachel and Mark's couch. Danny was active duty too, just waiting for new orders to come through. And hey, no one thought much of it at first.

But things escalated quickly. Within two weeks, Danny was hopping over to Trish's side of the duplex like it was a midnight relay race. At first, it was subtle—a cigarette on the shared back porch here, a "forgot something next door" there. But by week two, the porch light was flicking on and off like clockwork at 10 p.m., signaling his nightly trek to Trish's bedroom.

Of course, the neighbors noticed. "You think they're—?" Mrs. Cooper from two doors down whispered to Mrs. Jenkins. But the answer didn't take long to reveal itself. By month two, Trish was pregnant.

Now, let me tell you about Trish: the woman was a professional denier. She played it cool, walking the kids to the bus stop like her life wasn't a full-blown soap opera. Her bump? "Oh, just a little weight gain," she'd say with a laugh, brushing off the side-eyes and raised eyebrows. But anyone with eyes—and ears for the neighborhood gossip—knew what was really going on.

Ben, meanwhile, was blissfully unaware. Thanks to modern technology, they were video chatting once a month. "Hey babe," Trish cooed into the camera, her laptop carefully propped at the perfect angle to keep the bump out of sight. "The kids miss you so much."

And Ben? None the wiser. "I can't wait to get home," he said, grinning through the screen. Little did he know, Trish had other plans.

See, Trish wasn't just managing a secret affair and a pregnancy—she also had Power of Attorney. That meant she had full access to Ben's bank account, which she was steadily draining like a pro. New clothes for the kids? Sure. A little extra cash for late-night fast food runs with Danny? Why not? She even splurged on a few things she probably didn't need, like a fancy blender that sat untouched in the corner of the kitchen.

And then, two days before Ben was set to come home, Trish made her move. The U-Haul appeared in the driveway at sunrise, loaded with everything she could fit inside. The bump? She wasn't hiding it anymore. As she hauled boxes down the steps, one of the neighbors called out, "Moving already?"

Trish just smiled and waved. "Yep, family emergency!" she shouted back. No further explanation. By sunset, she was gone.

She didn't leave empty-handed, though. Oh no. On her way out of town, Trish cleaned out Ben's bank account. Every. Last. Cent. And as a final mic drop, she left her phone—dead, screen cracked—sitting on the kitchen counter. A goodbye note? Nah. That phone was all he was getting.

When Ben finally landed back stateside, he was probably picturing one of those tearful, sign-waving homecomings. What he got instead was an empty house, an empty bank account, and an empty marriage.

As for Trish? Rumor has it she and Danny rode off into the sunset together, but who knows? Maybe she's sipping margaritas on a beach somewhere, congratulating herself on pulling off one of the most audacious exit plans military housing has ever seen.

# Shelby

If you thought base housing was a hotbed of drama, let me introduce you to the wild world of military spouses with side hustles. It was 2017, maybe 2018, at Fort Bliss—a time when body sculpting was all the rage. And in the middle of this craze was Shelby. Ah, Shelby. A woman who thought, Why not take a hobby and turn it into an empire?

For those of you unfamiliar with body sculpting, let me clarify. We're not talking about clay or marble here. Body sculpting is one of those trendy, non-invasive beauty treatments where you're supposed to "melt away fat" or "tighten skin" using fancy equipment, freezing, or vibrations. It's the kind of thing Instagram influencers love to promote while pretending it's not a scam. And Shelby? She jumped on that bandwagon like it was her calling.

Spoiler alert: it didn't turn into an empire.

Shelby started small, posting announcements on social media about her "newfound passion" for sculpting bodies. And sure enough, women started booking appointments. Maybe they were curious, maybe they had too much time on their hands, or maybe they just wanted an excuse to gossip later. Whatever the reason, business picked up.

But not for the reasons you'd think.

You see, Shelby's name started popping up in group chats and spouse forums—not as a glowing recommendation, but as a cautionary tale. Because once you walked through the doors of Shelby's big house on the Northside, you realized things weren't exactly…professional.

Let me paint you a picture.

The house? Beautiful from the outside. It looked like the kind of place where you'd expect fresh-cut grass and a white picket fence. But inside? Oh, honey. Inside was another story entirely. The walls were chaos, the floors were a crime scene, and the decor was part "hoarder chic" and part "please call an exorcist." Let's not forget the pièce de résistance: the Koi Pond. Yes, a Koi Pond. In the living room. Except the water wasn't exactly crystal clear. It was green. Like, radioactive green. And whether the fish were alive or dead was anyone's guess. Maybe both?

But wait, there's more. Shelby had animals, too. Lots of them. Cats, dogs, maybe even a ferret or two—no one's sure because the smell hit you before you could start counting. There was shit everywhere. And I mean everywhere. It was as if the animals had collectively declared war on the concept of litter boxes.

And in the middle of this apocalyptic mess? Her body sculpting equipment. Just sitting there, like it wasn't completely surrounded by trash, animal droppings, and that ominous green glow from the Koi Pond. But don't worry—Shelby assured her clients she sanitized everything after every use. With what, you ask? Baby wipes. Because, in her words, "Clorox wipes are harmful to the body."

Now, look. I'm not here to debate the pros and cons of cleaning products, but let's all agree on one thing: if you're running a business involving people's bodies, baby wipes might not cut it.

Anyway, someone eventually had enough. Pictures of Shelby's setup started circulating, and before long, her husband's chain of command was involved. Because if there's one thing the military loves, it's being dragged into spouse drama. And let me tell you, Shelby's little operation was the kind of shitshow you couldn't ignore—literally.

But wait, there's one last plot twist. Shelby didn't just lose clients over her, uh, questionable practices. She also got herself kicked out of the spouse group. Why? Because, on top of everything else, Shelby was a racist. That's right. The woman who cleaned body sculpting tools with baby wipes while surrounded by Koi Pond sludge and animal shit somehow decided to throw bigotry into the mix. And that, folks, was the final nail in her social coffin.

So, what happened to Shelby? Well, she's still out there, selling her "services" to unsuspecting clients. Or not, maybe she's moved on to another hobby. One thing's for sure: Shelby will always be remembered as the cautionary tale of the body sculpting boom.

# Jennifer

Jennifer and John were high school sweethearts with big dreams. They married young, had their beautiful daughter Emma, and dove headfirst into military life. They were optimistic about the future, even when they moved into base housing. "It's not forever," Jennifer told herself. "We'll make it work."

But their home—if you could even call it that—was a nightmare from day one. Managed by Freedom Military Housing, the duplex looked decent enough on the outside. Fresh paint, clean landscaping—it could fool you at first glance. Inside, though, was a different story.

The first thing Jennifer noticed was the smell. It was the kind of damp, musty odor that clung to your clothes and made you question if it was safe to breathe. John, ever the optimist, waved it off. "Old pipes," he said, shrugging. But no amount of cleaning or air fresheners could mask the stench.

Then came the leaks. It didn't matter if it was raining or clear skies—water always seemed to find its way in. Buckets became a permanent fixture in their living room. The roof leaked, the windows leaked, and sometimes, Jennifer swore the walls were sweating. Maintenance was called over and over again, but the most they ever did was patch things up. Temporary fixes. Band-aids over bullet holes.

And the mold. Oh, the mold. It started in the bathroom, creeping up the walls in dark, spidery spots. Jennifer scrubbed and scrubbed, but it always came back. "It's nothing to worry about," the maintenance guy said, slapping a fresh coat of paint over the infestation. Two weeks later, it was back, spreading faster than before. Jennifer was terrified it would make Emma sick.

The plumbing wasn't much better. Faucets dripped, toilets backed up, and water pressure was a joke. "We're doing the best we can," the housing office told her, but Jennifer knew better. The best they could do was laughable.

Then there were the pests. Roaches, water bugs, and the occasional mouse made themselves at home. Jennifer once found a dead rat under the sink. "Just part of living in an older unit," the housing rep said with a forced smile. She wanted to scream.

The final straw came when Emma started coughing—deep, rattling coughs that wouldn't go away. Jennifer took her to the doctor, who confirmed her worst fear: mold exposure. Furious, she went back to the housing office, armed with medical records and photos of the mold. But the staff brushed her off, saying the problem wasn't "severe enough" to warrant relocation.

And then, just when Jennifer thought it couldn't get worse, the housing company changed names. Freedom Military Housing became Abraham Military Housing, and with that change came new promises. But those promises were empty. The houses stayed the same—or worse. "New name, same bullshit," Jennifer muttered under her breath as she watched another maintenance guy slap more paint over the mold.

Emma's cough got worse. Jennifer and John started sleeping in shifts, trying to keep the house as clean as possible. But it didn't matter. The house was toxic, literally and figuratively. And the worst part? They couldn't leave. They didn't have the money to move off base, and there were no other housing options available. They were stuck.

Jennifer joined a Facebook group for military spouses and quickly realized her family wasn't alone. Story after story flooded her social media feed. She saw families dealing with black mold, collapsing ceilings, infestations, and neglect. Some families had even sued, but the housing companies always seemed to win. It was like fighting a hydra—cut off one head, and two more grew in its place.

Despite the chaos, Jennifer tried to hold her family together. She kept calling, kept documenting, kept pushing for answers. But deep down, she knew it wouldn't change. The system was broken, and no amount of emails or angry phone calls could fix it.

Emma eventually recovered, but Jennifer would never forget the fear in those sleepless nights. Every time she looked at the walls of that house, she saw the cracks—literal and metaphorical. Cracks in the structure, cracks in the system, cracks in the promises made to families like hers.

Years later, Jennifer and John finally moved out. The day they left, she didn't look back. But she never stopped telling her story. "Don't let them gaslight you," she warned new military spouses. "If something's wrong, speak up. And don't believe for a second that a name change means things will get better."

Because sometimes, a fresh coat of paint and a shiny new name are just there to hide the rot underneath.

# Nina

Let's move on to a new story. Meet Nina, Sweet, patient, and probably a little too forgiving for her own good. She was the kind of wife who prided herself on being supportive, never saying no, and always keeping the spark alive in her marriage. Or so she thought.

It started one unsuspecting morning. Nina, half asleep and in desperate need of coffee, stumbled out of bed and headed to the kitchen. But as she passed the living room, she caught sight of something that stopped her dead in her tracks. There he was—her husband—on the couch, pants around his ankles, mid-jerk.

"Uh...what the actual fuck?" Nina blurted out, startling him so badly that he nearly fell off the couch.

Caught. Red-handed. Literally.

He scrambled to cover himself, stammering out excuses like a teenager caught stealing beer from the fridge. "I...I didn't know you were up," he sputtered, his face flushing a shade of crimson she'd never seen before. Nina just stared, too stunned to even process what was happening.

"Okay, seriously," she said, crossing her arms. "What the fuck are you doing?"

And this man—her husband, the father of her children, the guy who promised to love her forever—looked her dead in the eye and said, "I was tired of getting a woodie at PT in the morning."

She blinked. "You...what?"

"PT," he repeated as if that clarified anything. "It's embarrassing. I needed to…take care of it."

Nina didn't know whether to laugh, scream, or throw something. "Are you seriously telling me you're doing this because of PT? At six in the morning? On the fucking couch?"

"I was gonna clean up!" he protested as if that made it better.

Now, here's the thing about Nina: she's not the jealous type. She doesn't snoop, doesn't question, doesn't accuse. She's always been the "cool wife." But something about this whole situation didn't sit right with her. And as the days went on, little things started to click. Like how her husband had been extra distant lately. Or how he suddenly started taking his phone with him everywhere, even to the bathroom. Or how he always seemed to have a stupid grin on his face after work, like he knew something she didn't.

Then came the bombshell.

It didn't take long for Nina to find out the truth: her husband had been cheating on her. And not just with some random fling—oh no. He was fucking around with a woman he worked with. The kind of woman Nina had met at office BBQs and FRG meetings, the one who smiled too wide and laughed too hard at his dumb jokes. That's who he'd been fantasizing about that morning on the couch.

To say Nina was livid would be an understatement. She confronted him, of course, and true to form, he played dumb. "It's not what it looks like!" he insisted, even as the evidence piled up like dirty laundry.

"Oh, really?" Nina snapped. "Then explain why you're on the couch thinking about her while I'm upstairs asleep, you fucking idiot."

He didn't have an answer for that.

Nina, being the badass she is, didn't waste time wallowing. She packed his shit, threw it on the lawn, and made it clear he wasn't welcome back

And just like that, Nina became another cautionary tale in the wild world of military marriage. But don't feel too bad for her—she's thriving now. New job, new house, new boyfriend who *actually* respects her. And as for her ex? Well, he got kicked out of the military and is living the bum life now.

# Earl Gray

Okay, pause for a second. Let's be honest here—if you've spent more than five minutes around the military community, you've probably heard the stereotype: the military is crawling with cheaters. It's practically a meme at this point. You know, the kind of thing people laugh about in dark corners of Facebook groups: "Oh, he's deploying? Better keep an eye on his phone." "She's in the FRG? Say goodbye to fidelity." It's all fun and games…until it's not. Until it's real.

Because here's the truth: it's not just a punchline. It's people's lives. And it's messy. Like, reality-show-level messy. We're talking secrets, betrayals, and enough drama to fuel a thousand group chats. And if you think that's an exaggeration? Oh, honey. You're in for a ride.

Here's the kicker, though: everything you've read so far? Every ridiculous, infuriating, jaw-dropping story? It's true. Every. Single. One. People sent these stories to me—some anonymously, others with zero shame and a "Hell yeah, use my name" attitude. But here's the deal: no names in this book are real. I allowed each person to choose the names for their story. So if you find some repeating names, blame their lack of creativity, not mine. I did the name changes for a reason, not because I don't want to throw people under the bus (let's be honest, some of them deserve it), but because this isn't about revenge. It's about truth. And honestly, some of these stories are so wild, that you don't even need real names to believe them.

Think about it: how many times have you heard about someone's spouse going "back home" for no reason, or that one FRG meeting that turned into a soap opera, or the "buddy" who's always just a little too close? You hear these stories, you roll your eyes, you laugh, but deep down, you know there's a kernel of truth in all of it. That's what this is—just kernels of truth wrapped up in a big ol' burrito of drama.

And listen, I get it. It's easy to sit back and judge. "That would never happen to me," you think. But let me tell you, military life has a way of throwing curveballs you never see coming. One minute, you're baking cookies for the squadron, and the next, you're calling the base legal office because your neighbor found your husband's Grinder profile. Trust me, no one is immune.

So here's your reminder: what you're reading isn't fiction. These aren't made-up characters in some trashy novel. These are real people, with real stories, living real lives. And honestly? That's what makes it all so compelling. Because as ridiculous as it all sounds, it's true. Every name, every detail, every heartbreak and scandal, it's real. Well, except the names. I had everyone change those because I'm not trying to start World War III in someone's base housing neighborhood.

Buckle up, my friend. If you think it's been a wild ride so far, you're not ready for what's coming next. Spoiler alert: it involves even more drama, even more WTF moments, and just enough humor to keep you from throwing this book across the room. Let's keep going. It's about to get better.

# Laura

Our next story is all about Laura. Laura was the resident military spouse photographer, running a little operation called "Click Click Photos." Her business promised family portraits that would make your friends jealous and your Instagram pop.

It all started innocently enough. Laura would post in spouse groups: "Mini sessions this weekend! Affordable prices! Quick turnaround!" And because military families love a deal and a good photo op, people flocked to her. But here's the thing: Laura's promises rarely, if ever, matched reality.

For starters, Laura's punctuality was...let's just say, optional. Families would arrive at their designated spots—parks, beaches, backyards—ready to smile for the camera. But instead of Laura, they'd be greeted by an empty scene and the slow realization that they'd been ghosted. Eventually, Laura would show up, often with a flustered apology. "Traffic was insane!" or "I couldn't find my camera bag!" (Yes, her camera bag—not a great thing to misplace for a photographer.) By the time she was ready to start, kids were cranky, parents were annoyed, and the sunlight was disappearing fast.

But even when she was on time, Laura had a knack for derailing her own sessions. She loved to chat, often veering into personal overshares about her housing drama, her ex-boyfriend's texts, or why she hated her neighbors. Meanwhile, kids squirmed, parents tried to maintain smiles, and everyone silently wondered, "Is this part of the package?"

Then there was her editing—or as one client put it, "the crime scene cleanup." Laura promised quick turnarounds, but her idea of "quick" was...elastic. A week became a month, and a month became three. When families finally got their photos, they were hit with the realization that Laura's editing skills were, uh, unique. Overexposed shots, weird filters, and lighting that made them look like they were glowing from within. One mom joked that her toddler looked like he belonged in a sci-fi movie.

And then, there was the stock photo incident. At some point, clients started noticing something odd about Laura's portfolio. Like, why did her "family beach session" include people wearing snow boots? Turns out, Laura had been padding her portfolio with images that weren't hers. When confronted, she claimed they were "inspiration." Yeah, sure, Laura.

The breaking point for many came when Laura's excuses started piling up like laundry in a deployment household. The computer broke. The camera broke. The dog ate her SD card (okay, not really, but it might as well have been). Clients were ghosted entirely. At some point, someone reported her to the group admins, and Laura's name became the stuff of legend: "Don't book Click Click Photos unless you want a blurry shot of your kid looking miserable."

Laura eventually disappeared from the local scene. But not for long. Like a phoenix rising from the ashes of overexposed photos, she rebranded under a new name. "Snap Snap Memories," "Shutter Bliss Studios," and "Perfect Portraits" all appeared in quick succession.

Each time, the same cycle repeated: glowing promises, chaotic sessions, and disappointed families.

Where is Laura now? No one knows for sure, she's probably advertising "limited edition mini sessions" in some new military town. But wherever she is, I hope she's figured out how to keep track of her camera bag—and maybe left the stock photos behind.

*Let Laura's story serve as a gentle reminder: not all photographers are created equal. Do your research, ask for referrals, and for the love of everything holy, never pay in advance. Otherwise, you might just end up with photos that look like they were taken through a Snapchat filter by a distracted toddler.*

# Abigail

Picture this: a quiet military base where the most exciting thing on a Thursday afternoon is the sound of lawnmowers and a neighborhood kid wiping out on a scooter. But all that peace ended the moment Abigail looked out her window and saw an unexpected visitor in her driveway.

Now, Abigail wasn't someone who let things go. She grabbed her phone, recorded the mess, and, like any military spouse with a plan, went straight to Facebook. Her post was pure passive-aggressive gold:

"To the lady whose dog killed the chicken in my driveway. I told you to take care of it. If you're not back to deal with this by the time I get home, I'm posting the video and putting you on blast."

Simple. Clear. Just the right amount of threatening. And it worked—people started commenting faster than if she'd posted a giveaway. Within minutes, the spouse group was buzzing, turning one dead chicken into the kind of drama people live for.

Vanessa, the dog's owner, was the first to reply. "I understand it's on us that the dog got out," she said, trying to sound calm. "But you don't need to be rude. We've already called maintenance to come pick it up."

Maintenance. She called maintenance. For a chicken. Abigail could feel her blood boiling as comments started pouring in:

"Maintenance? Really?"

"Why not just deal with it yourself?"

"This is why everyone hates living on base."

Vanessa wasn't done. She added, "It's not the dog's fault—it's just what they do!" That didn't help. Someone replied, "Then keep your dog on a leash if that's what they do."

Meanwhile, Patricia joined the fight. Patricia was the kind of person who couldn't help but share her opinion, even when no one asked for it. "If you can't control your animals, you shouldn't have them," she wrote, probably while sipping coffee in her spotless living room.

Abigail wasn't backing down. She shot back:

"You can delete your comments all you want, but the video shows everything. Either you come clean this up, or I'll leave it on your porch."

The group was eating it up. Someone commented, "Post the video!" followed by another, "Yes, post it!" Abigail was tempted—so tempted. But she wasn't ready to go nuclear. Not yet.

Then someone shifted the focus: "Why is there a chicken on base anyway? This isn't a farm." Another chimed in, "Who has loose dogs and chickens? This is the most ridiculous thing I've seen."

And then, in the wildest twist, someone casually admitted, "My dog's killed chickens before. It's annoying, but you just bag it up and throw it away." Like it was nothing. Abigail was floored. Bag it up? Throw it away? Like it was some old leftovers?

By the end of the day, Vanessa finally came over and picked up what was left of the chicken, but not without making it clear she felt like the victim. Abigail didn't post the video, but you'd better believe she saved it—just in case Vanessa's dog decided to cause more problems.

Let's be real—base housing drama is its own kind of sport. It's a little petty, a little funny, and a whole lot messy. Abigail's story proves one thing: even a chicken can turn a quiet neighborhood into a full-blown war. Whether it's dogs, chickens, or calling maintenance for things you can deal with yourself, base housing drama never fails.

# Callie

Let me tell you about the neighbor from hell.

It all started at Fort Bliss, in one of those overpriced "luxury" apartments that should really be called "moldy overpriced nightmares." You know the ones—where the walls are thin enough to hear your neighbor sneeze, but management swears it's high-end living.

Callie and her family were military too, and I was actually excited. A fellow spouse! A potential friend! She even had a toddler around my son's age. It was like the universe was giving me a little mom buddy. Or so I thought.

I smiled at her one day in the hall, gave her the friendliest, warmest hello I could muster. You know what she did? She scoffed. Not a polite nod, not an "Oh, hey." Just a scoff and a dramatic turn away, like I'd personally offended her existence. Fantastic. Just the connection I was hoping for.

Still, I brushed it off. Maybe she was having a bad day. We've all been there, right? But then, one day, while I was making lunch and my son was napping, I heard it. A blood-curdling scream. The kind of scream that makes your stomach drop and your brain go into overdrive. I grabbed my—you know, home-defense pew pew—because what if something was really wrong?

I ran upstairs and knocked on their door. Her husband answered, looking half asleep. "Hey, I heard a noise," I said, trying to sound casual while secretly imagining all kinds of crime scene scenarios. He shrugged and told me his wife screamed at their daughter, who was crying because she was sick.

Now, let me be clear: I don't judge moms. Ever. Crying kids, messy houses, days where you're just barely hanging on? Been there. But screaming like a banshee at a sick toddler? That's a new level. I walked back to my apartment in disbelief, questioning all my life choices that led me to this moment.

And then, just when I thought things couldn't get weirder, they did.

One night, my husband and I were in our bedroom watching a movie when we heard it. The noises. And not the toddler-throwing-a-tantrum kind. Oh no. This was...different. Let's just say Callie was having the time of her life. It was like something out of a romance novel, except louder. And there was one glaring problem: her husband wasn't home. He was in the field.

Naturally, my nosy self had to investigate. I peeked out the window and, sure enough, there was an unfamiliar car parked out front. Christian Grey, is that you?

Her husband came back from the field a few days later, none the wiser. I wanted so badly to say something, he was genuinely one of the sweetest guys I'd ever met. But, Callie was...intimidating. The kind of person you just knew would throw hands without hesitation.

So, instead of confronting her directly, I went to the apartment office. I casually mentioned the noise and suggested they let the husband know when it happened. The office staff looked devastated for the guy, but who knows if they ever actually said anything.

A few weeks later, we moved out, and I thought I'd seen the last of Callie. But, of course, the drama wasn't done yet. Right before we left, I saw her, belly the size of a basketball. She was pregnant again. The only question on everyone's mind: Who's the daddy? Her husband? The mysterious car guy? We'll never know.

# Susie

Lets set the stage: a quiet military base, a suspicious husband, a certain chain restaurant, and enough drama to make Jerry Springer look tame. This isn't your average cheating story, it's a Chili's special.

This story begins with a husband—let's call him Ben. Ben is calm, sweet, and, by all accounts, a decent guy who loves his wife to a fault. But even Ben can only take so much, and after hearing rumors about his wife's extracurricular activities, he went full detective. Armed with some very incriminating photos from a "helpful" anonymous source, Ben found himself walking into the local Chili's. Not for bottomless chips and salsa, but to ask the manager a simple, loaded question: "Can I see your security footage?"

Why? Because his wife, Susie, had told him she was at work that day. Spoiler alert: she wasn't. And while Susie was supposed to be clocked in somewhere respectable, she was instead at Chili's—sneaking around with a man who most definitely wasn't Ben. Let's call him Dave, because Dave just sounds like the kind of guy who'd roll up to a family restaurant thinking he's smooth.

Now, Ben's not your typical jealous husband. He wasn't stomping around, yelling, or demanding justice on the spot. No, this man was calm. Too calm. According to witnesses, his aura (yes, aura) radiated a kind of eerie, cold determination. It was the kind of energy that says, "I'm not mad; I'm just planning your downfall." Honestly? It was terrifying.

Meanwhile, Susie was living her best sneaky life. She was supposed to be at work but had decided Chili's was the perfect place to cuddle up with Dave. Now, I don't know about you, but if I were going to risk blowing up my marriage, I'd at least pick somewhere a little less...chain-y. But hey, to each their own.

The kicker? Susie and Dave didn't even try to be subtle. Not only were they spotted at Chili's, but they also left together in his car. And, of course, Ben made it his mission to track down the license plate. This man was playing chess while everyone else was playing checkers.

And then there's the plot twist no one saw coming: instead of blowing up on Susie, Ben blamed himself. Himself! This man, who had done nothing wrong, was out here saying,

"Maybe it's my fault."

**Excuse me, what?**

Ben, sweetie, no. Just because Susie decided to trade in her loyalty for a two-for-one fajita deal doesn't mean this is on you. But Ben, ever the gentleman, couldn't see it that way. Instead, he spent his time praising Susie's accomplishments, telling everyone how amazing and kind she was. Honestly, the guy deserves a medal—or at least a hug.

Now, let's talk about Dave. Dave, who clearly missed the memo that wedding rings mean hands off, was out here acting like he'd won some kind of prize. Spoiler alert: when the prize is someone else's wife, it's not really a win. The audacity of this man to not only chase after Susie but to do it publicly? Chef's kiss. The drama writes itself.

As for Susie, she was as bold as they come. The woman didn't even try to cover her tracks. Someone suggested to Ben that he should leave her, and all I could think was, "There's a line of women who'd happily take his place."

And let's not forget the bystanders who couldn't help but chime in. "Why Chili's?" someone asked. "Couldn't she at least cheat with some class?" Another person added, "Dave better watch out. Karma's coming for him, and she doesn't mess around."

Military life has its fair share of drama, but this? This was a whole soap opera set in the most unexpected place. Ben, if you're reading this, focus on yourself. Stop blaming yourself for someone else's bad choices. You deserve better.

Susie, if you don't want to be with your husband, at least have the guts to say it. Don't drag him through this mess.

And Dave? Buddy, you dodged a bullet this time, but don't push your luck. Karma has a long memory, and she's got a Chili's receipt with your name on it.

# Jasmine Tea

If you haven't had the pleasure of spending time with a military kid, you're missing out on some of the best comedy life has to offer. These little human tornadoes are a perfect mix of too-smart-for-their-own-good and way-too-comfortable-with-chaos. They've been through more duty stations than most adults, and their perspective on life? Well, let's just say it's a blend of wisdom and pure comedic gold.

Take Mikey, a five-year-old who recently attended his dad's reenlistment ceremony. While everyone else stood tall and solemn, Mikey turned to his mom, face serious, and asked, "Does this mean Daddy has to go back to the desert and play hide-and-seek again?" You could practically hear the crowd biting back their laughter while his dad tried to keep his composure. Honestly, Mikey? Nailed it.

Then there's Olivia, the seven-year-old philosopher. She confidently told her entire second-grade class that her mom, who is deployed, "is like a ninja but cooler because ninjas don't have jets." When her teacher tried to explain that jets aren't typically silent like ninjas, Olivia didn't miss a beat. "Yeah, but they go 'whoosh,' and that's a cooler sound anyway." Touché, Olivia.

Of course, military kids are also known for their no-filter honesty. Nine-year-old Ethan, for example, recently sat through a base housing tour with his parents. After seeing a suspiciously patched-up wall, he whispered (loud enough for everyone to hear), "Is this where the last people punched it because they hated it here?" Ethan's dad turned bright red, but let's be real—Ethan just said what we're all thinking during those tours.

And then there's Emma, a precocious ten-year-old who decided to get crafty for her deployed mom. She mailed her mom a homemade "deployment survival kit" that included essentials like a rubber band ball, five packets of ketchup from McDonald's, and a note that said, "Don't get lost. Her mom loved it.

But my favorite might just be twelve-year-old Lucas, who was asked to write about his hero for a school assignment. While other kids picked athletes or fictional characters, Lucas wrote a heartfelt essay about his big sister, who had just joined the Navy. "She's brave and strong, but she's also really bad at texting back," he wrote. "That's okay, though. She's busy saving the world or something." I mean, come on—how do you not tear up and laugh at the same time?

Military kids are also masters of adaptation. They can pack their lives into a moving box faster than most of us can pack a suitcase. Little Ellie, age six, recently informed her teacher that her family doesn't live anywhere—they just "borrow houses until it's someone else's turn." When asked if that made her sad, she shrugged.

"Not really. We always get new neighbors to spy on."

Someone get this girl a detective badge.

And let's not forget about their vocabulary. These kids throw around words like "PCS" and "TAD" like they're part of the alphabet song. Six-year-old Grayson recently explained to his soccer coach that his dad couldn't make it to practice because he was

"TDY to fix some classified stuff."

The coach nodded like he understood, but Grayson could tell.

"It's okay," he added, patting the coach's arm. "It just means he's busy being a hero."

Honestly, put that on a Hallmark card.

At the end of the day, military kids are a breed of their own. They're resilient, hilarious, and wise beyond their years. They might not always say the right thing, but they always say the most memorable thing. And for that, we salute them.

# Stephanie

So, my friend Stephanie texted me the other day, something that perfectly sums up the unique blend of ego, denial, and hilarity that comes with military spouse life.

So, Stephanie and two other spouses—let's call them Lisa and Karen—were all in the same neighborhood, all with husbands deployed at the same time. Naturally, this meant plenty of "deployment bonding sessions," which usually involved coffee, gossip, and the occasional rant about household projects that would mysteriously remain unfinished even after their husbands came home.

One day, while hanging out with Lisa and Karen, Stephanie did what any normal person would do—she asked how everyone's husbands were doing. You know, checking in, sharing updates, the usual.

Lisa, whose husband was in a completely different country, kept it short and sweet: "He's good. Same old, same old."

But Karen? Oh, Karen. She leaned in with a conspiratorial whisper and said,

"Oh, my husband's on a special training mission. It's super classified, so he can't have his phone. I'm not allowed to talk about it."

Stephanie blinked. Special training mission? Classified? Her husband, who was on the same deployment, had never mentioned anything remotely special—or classified, for that matter. But hey, who was she to question Karen's James Bond fantasy?

Later that day, Stephanie casually brought it up to her husband during one of their daily calls.

"Hey, is Karen's husband with you?"

"Oh, yeah," her husband replied, chuckling. "We had chow together today. He's sleeping on the ground next to us, same as everyone else."

Stephanie couldn't help but laugh. So much for the "special training mission." The guy wasn't exactly storming enemy compounds or decoding top-secret files—he was eating MREs and roughing it in the dirt like the rest of them.

Now, here's the thing, Karen wasn't just a regular military spouse. She was one of *those* spouses. You know the type. FRG queen, always acting like her husband was ten ranks higher than he actually was, and constantly trying to one-up everyone else. So, of course, the idea that her husband was doing something extraordinary fit right into her narrative.

Stephanie didn't call her out—what was the point? But every time Karen brought up her husband's "classified work," Stephanie had to fight the urge to laugh. Because let's be real: the only thing "special" about his deployment was how quickly Karen had convinced herself he was some kind of military superhero.

*Military life has a way of turning even the most mundane things into epic tales of drama and delusion. Karen's story is a classic example of how some people just can't resist making everything about them.*

*And hey, maybe it's harmless. But the next time someone starts talking about "classified missions," just remember: there's a good chance their husband is sitting in a tent somewhere, complaining about how the Wi-Fi doesn't work.*

# Hannah

Picture this: a crisp winter afternoon at Fort Cavazos—previously Fort Hood, but we don't talk about that. Neighbors are sipping lukewarm coffee, kids are screaming like banshees, and somewhere in this peaceful chaos, there's a backyard drama brewing that would make *Jerry Springer* weep.

At the center of it all? Hannah. Hannah is a woman on a mission. Not one to be babysat by "nervous Nancies," she proudly lets her two-year-old frolic in the backyard *unsupervised* while her German shepherd, Xena, keeps watch. This ain't no quiet little toddler nap situation, oh no. Hannah is proudly throwing open every door and window of her house while scrubbing it down like she's about to host the base commander for dinner.

Now, here's the thing about the military spouse community: everyone watches *everything*. Someone sneezes weird, and suddenly it's in the Facebook group with 60 comments debating the sneeze

So, naturally, when little Timmy (let's call him Timmy) was outside "without his skin"—as Hannah put it—every Karen, Becky, and Nancy came crawling out of the woodwork, ready to blow the whistle.

"Without his skin?!" one horrified neighbor typed, fingers probably shaking. "Does she mean naked?! Someone call CPS!"

Now, was Timmy naked? No. But Hannah's poetic phrasing sent imaginations running wild. And suddenly, Fort Cavazos' local Facebook group was *lit*.

One neighbor, let's call her Linda, fired the first shot. "Your kid is *two,* Hannah. You're lucky he hasn't been scooped up by fire ants, stray dogs, or a rogue wind gust. *You're sick.*"

Hannah, bless her Texas-born heart, was not about to take this lying down. "First of all, *hunnay*," she typed, probably snapping her fingers IRL, "I've been here since it was Fort Hood, and my son ain't too much for me to handle. I don't need *anyone* telling me how to raise my child, so you can sit down."

And just like that, it was on. Comments were flying faster than kids on a sugar high. Someone brought up child neglect. Another suggested fire ants were lurking. A quiet voice in the back (let's call her Yellow Shirt) chimed in: "I like when y'all fight. Keeps me entertained while I'm nap trapped."

But the MVP? The anonymous commenter who broke it down for the confused souls: *"Without me in his skin" = without me being glued to him like Velcro, not without clothes, people. Chill.*

You'd think that would end it, right? Oh no. Another neighbor in green chimed in, *"People are way too sensitive. Calm down, her dog probably had it handled."* To which Linda screamed into the void: "YOU CANNOT LET A DOG BABYSIT A CHILD."

And Hannah? Hannah wasn't done. "Back in my day, we lived on 40 acres and kids were fine. I don't know what kind of childhood y'all had, but I ain't helicoptering around my kid."

By this point, the thread was hotter than a Texas summer. A self-proclaimed social worker (probably named Brenda) tried to bring in some professionalism. "There are *rules,* you know. Legally, kids under 10 shouldn't be unattended." But before Brenda could adjust her reading glasses, another Karen accused her of reading at a 6th-grade level, and it was every woman for herself.

In the background, I imagine Hannah sipping her sweet tea, watching the chaos she created like Thanos admiring his work. Timmy was back inside, Xena was taking a nap, and the entire group was now divided between Team *"Hannah's a negligent mom"* and Team *"Let the woman live!"*

What did we learn from all this? Nothing, really. But it's a timeless truth: never underestimate the power of a bored neighborhood and a Facebook group.

And to all the Karens out there: if you're going to call someone out, make sure you don't misspell "bachelor's degree."

# Melody

Alright, y'all, grab your Tea and settle in, because this one is about to ruin your morning brew forever.

Meet Melody, the military spouse who decided her estranged Air Force husband, Roby, was better off six feet under than in divorce court. And her weapon of choice, the coffee pot. Because if there's one thing Melody believed in, it's starting your day strong—*and maybe dead.*

Roby and Melody were stationed overseas in Germany. Things in their marriage were already circling the drain. Divorce papers were in motion, tensions were high, and Melody—oh, sweet Melody—decided to take matters into her own *toxic* hands.

One morning, Roby's coffee started tasting… *weird.* Now, if you're military, you're used to drinking things that could probably peel paint off the walls—barracks coffee, anyone? But this, this was different. It wasn't just burnt or bitter; it had a certain… *chemical tang.* Roby, being a seasoned Air Force man, didn't chalk it up to a bad roast. Nope, he sniffed trouble.

Roby went out and got some pool chlorine test strips. Yes, you read that right. My man straight-up CSI'd his kitchen. He tested his morning brew like it was a scene out of *Breaking Bad*, and BAM—there it was: chlorine. Enough to make a pool inspector weep. This wasn't a mistake. This wasn't an "oops, I used the wrong creamer." This was deliberate.

Now, I know what you're thinking: *He confronted her, right?* Nope. Roby went full special ops. Instead of flipping the table and yelling,

"WHY ARE YOU TRYING TO KILL ME, MELODY?!"

he calmly set up hidden cameras. Because nothing says "military spouse drama" like catching your wife red-handed via spy cam. And oh, she delivered. The cameras caught Melody sneaking into the kitchen and pouring bleach into the coffee pot like she was topping off a fancy cocktail.

You'd think it would stop there. But nope. When Roby finally managed to get them moved stateside—to Davis-Monthan Air Force Base in Arizona—he brought the footage to the police. And this is where it gets *even crazier*. The authorities were like, "Hmm, interesting. But we're gonna need more proof." Because apparently, one video of your wife spiking your coffee with industrial chemicals isn't *enough*.

So Roby doubled down. More cameras. More angles. He caught Melody sneaking bleach from the laundry room, walking it back to the kitchen, and doing her best mad scientist impression. And meanwhile, Roby—bless him—continued to *pretend* to drink the coffee every single morning. Can you imagine the guts that takes? Sitting across from your wife at breakfast, smiling while sipping from a cup you know could send you to the afterlife? This man deserves a medal.

Finally, the police couldn't ignore the evidence anymore. Melody was arrested on charges of **aggravated assault** and **adding harmful substances to food or drink**—which is the most polite legal term for "tried to poison her husband to death." But here's where I scream into the void: Melody *pleaded guilty*, and her punishment? Three years of **probation**. Let that sink in. I can't jaywalk without a cop side-eyeing me, but she got probation for turning her husband's coffee into a *chlorine smoothie*. Justice? Not sure I know her.

And why'd she do it, you ask? Well, Melody was allegedly hoping to collect Roby's death benefits. Yep. She really thought her husband's life insurance payout was going to be her ticket to freedom. But instead of cashing in, she got caught, embarrassed on a national scale, and turned into the punchline of every "crazy spouse" story told over base BBQs.

So here's the moral of the story:

1. If your coffee tastes even slightly like a public pool, *do not drink it.*
2. Never underestimate the ingenuity of a military spouse with a grudge, a coffee maker, and a misplaced sense of ambition.
3. And most importantly? If your marriage ever gets so bad you start Googling "how to poison my spouse," just... don't. Divorce might be expensive, but murder-by-poison is *so* much worse for your resume.

Now go enjoy your coffee, folks. And maybe pour it yourself.

# Sasha

The audacity of men like Preston is unmatched.

Picture this: Sasha—married for over a decade, raising her daughter Olivia, who's now 19, ready to take on the world. Sasha worked *hard* to make life good. She's a straight-shooter, the kind of woman who makes dinner on time, keeps her house spotless, and still manages to look put together when running errands on base. A true military spouse veteran. And Preston? Oh, he was your typical midlife-crisis-having doofus. You know the type: a little too attached to his Bluetooth headset, too much cologne for a grown man, and perpetually whining about "needing space."

But nothing—and I mean *nothing*—could have prepared Sasha for *this*.

It all started when Sasha's phone dinged with a text from a friend. Kendra, who lived for the base gossip, had sent a screenshot of a post so vile Sasha almost dropped her coffee. The anonymous post read:

"So I'm an active-duty service member, married to a woman with a daughter who's now 19. She's not my biological daughter, but we've fallen in love. My question is—if I leave my wife and marry her daughter, is it difficult to transfer Tricare over to her as my wife? I'm worried because she may be pregnant."

Sasha blinked. Stared. Re-read it. The words didn't change.

"Kendra, is this a joke?" she texted back.

Kendra's response came immediately: "Girl, I wish. This was posted an hour ago. You don't think... it's Preston, do you?"

Sasha's blood turned ice cold. Because while Preston *was* a walking red flag, this level of scumbaggery hadn't even occurred to her.

But suddenly, a lot of little things started adding up.

You see, Preston had been acting shady for months. It started with the weird comments about Olivia. Things like, "Wow, she's really grown up, huh?" and "You're lucky, Sasha. Olivia's so mature for her age." At the time, Sasha brushed it off as Preston being his usual awkward self, but now? Now she wanted to throw up.

Then there were the late-night conversations. Preston would "help" Olivia with things like her car or her college assignments, sitting on the couch with her while Sasha pretended to ignore the weird tension. Olivia didn't seem to notice anything—she was a kid at heart, bright-eyed and ambitious, too busy planning her future to pick up on Preston's creep vibes.

But Sasha? Oh, Sasha noticed.

It hit her all at once. She remembered the brand-new iPad Preston had gifted Olivia "just because." The random coffee dates he would "treat" her to without inviting Sasha along. The gym trips where Preston said he was "mentoring" young airmen, but in reality, he was probably out somewhere rehearsing his role as the villain of a telenovela.

Sasha didn't play games, so that evening, she decided to confront Preston. She made his favorite dinner—grilled steak, homemade bread rolls, and mashed potatoes—and waited for him to walk through the door.

As Preston dropped his gym bag on the floor and plopped onto the couch, Sasha walked up with her phone in hand.

"Preston," she said calmly, "you got anything to tell me?"

Preston looked up, chewing a piece of bread like he didn't have a care in the world. "What do you mean?"

Sasha smiled—*the* smile. You know, the one that says *you've got five seconds to come clean before I burn your life down.*

She shoved the phone into his hands. "Read. It."

Preston's face went pale. "W-what is this?"

"Something a little too familiar, don't you think? Oh, and before you lie, I want you to consider the fact that I can access the phone records. I'm not stupid, Preston."

He tried to laugh it off, like some man-child caught with his hand in the cookie jar.

"Sasha, come on. That's *not* me. I'd never—"

Sasha held up a hand.

"Stop. I've ignored too many signs already. You've been hanging around Olivia like she's your girlfriend, buying her gifts, taking her out—are you going to tell me it's all innocent? Because *nothing* about this feels innocent."

Preston's excuses sputtered out like a bad car engine, and Sasha had seen enough. He stammered, and tried to play it off, but Sasha had already made up her mind.

"Pack a bag," she said evenly. "I want you out of my house tonight."

She expected Olivia to be just as disgusted. She expected her daughter to be furious, to cut him off just as quickly. But Olivia? Olivia hesitated.

"I mean…" Olivia trailed off, suddenly avoiding Sasha's eyes. "He treats me really well."

It took a second for the words to register. Sasha's heart sank. Preston didn't just *think* he was in love with Olivia. Olivia had *fallen for him too*. And worse? She was pregnant. Sasha was devastated. She begged Olivia to see reason, to recognize how *wrong* this was. But love—especially the kind wrapped up in manipulation—doesn't listen to logic.

In the end, Olivia made her choice. She packed her things and left with Preston.

The base was in an uproar. Gossip spread like wildfire. Preston was *that guy* now—the one who ran off with his stepdaughter and had the audacity to try and make it official. He requested a transfer to another unit, but his reputation followed him.

And Sasha? She grieved. Not for Preston—he wasn't worth a second thought—but for Olivia. Olivia, who had been so young, so trusting. Olivia, who now had a baby on the way with a man old enough to know better. Olivia, who, despite everything, still believed this was love.

Months later, Sasha heard through the grapevine that Olivia and Preston had officially tied the knot. They had moved off base, starting fresh somewhere no one knew them. Sasha didn't reach out. She couldn't. It hurt too much. Instead, she focused on herself—on healing, on moving forward. Occasionally, she'd scroll through military spouse groups just to watch the drama unfold from a safe distance.

Let this be a lesson: Some men will do anything for a fresh start, but that doesn't mean it's right. And if you put your wildest thoughts on the internet, don't be surprised when the internet *never forgets.*

# Stacy

The name Stacy alone sparks whispers around base, accompanied by smirks, eye rolls, and the occasional hushed "bless her heart." See, Stacy isn't just any barracks bunny. Oh no. Stacy has a plan. A big, ambitious, and slightly tragic plan: snag herself a military man. Why? Two words—Tricare benefits.

Now, before you judge, let me paint you a picture. Stacy didn't grow up dreaming of white picket fences or a respectable 9-to-5. She didn't care about the medals pinned on a uniform or the prestige of being a military wife. What Stacy *did* care about, however, was stability—and in her mind, a husband in uniform meant health insurance, steady paychecks, and an end to the chaos she grew up in. Romantic? No. Practical? Very.

And thus began her unofficial mission: Operation Bag-A-Benefits.

**Room 101: Kyle – The Slob**

Stacy's first target—if you can call him that—was Kyle. Kyle, whose room looked like a landfill had set up shop between four walls. Stacy stood in the doorway, mentally hyping herself up. She wasn't here for the ambiance. She was here for *opportunity*.

"Hey," Kyle grunted, waving a beer can in her general direction.

Stacy plastered on a smile, ignoring the carpet of crumpled Chipotle wrappers. "Mind if I come in?"

Kyle shrugged, already halfway through a *Call of Duty* match. His mattress didn't have a sheet, his socks were sticky, and his trash can was overflowing. Stacy stepped over a suspicious stain on the floor and perched herself on the corner of the bed, grimacing internally.

This wasn't about love. It wasn't even about like. It was survival. If she could deal with her ex's broken-down Chevy and questionable hygiene, she could deal with Kyle. Unfortunately, Kyle's big selling point—being in the Navy—came with a huge downside: he didn't *want* Stacy. Not really. He barely noticed when she was there, too busy staring at the TV or double-fisting Doritos.

When Stacy finally left the next morning, hair in a messy bun and pride hanging by a thread, she muttered under her breath, "Next."

**Room 103: Brandon – Mr. OCD**

Brandon was Stacy's second stop, and to her credit, she put on her best "girl next door" act for this one. Brandon was neat. Military precision neat. Shoes lined up, bed perfectly made, uniform hung like a museum piece.

"Shoes off," Brandon barked the second Stacy stepped inside. "Don't touch the desk."

Stacy rolled her eyes but obliged, because *this one* had potential. He wasn't much of a charmer, but he was clean, organized, and already showed a deep commitment to folding towels perfectly in thirds—qualities Stacy assumed would transfer well into "husband material."

They hooked up, and afterward, while Brandon straightened a rogue crease in his blanket, Stacy tried to plant seeds. "You ever think about settling down? You know, getting married?"

Brandon looked horrified. "I'm 22."

"Yeah, but..." Stacy pushed. "Wouldn't it be nice to have someone waiting for you after deployment?"

Brandon nodded thoughtfully before replying, "Sure. I'll probably marry a pilot or something."

Stacy left with a forced smile and muttered yet again, "Next."

## Room 107: Jeremy – The Angry Drunk

Desperation is a slippery slope, and by the time Stacy found herself in Jeremy's room, she'd already resigned herself to playing defense. Jeremy was angry at *everything*. His CO, the vending machine, his ex-girlfriend, the wind—didn't matter. Stacy sat there, nodding politely while Jeremy went on a whiskey-fueled rant about how the Navy ruined his life.

"I don't need a woman anyway," Jeremy spat, pounding his fist on the desk for emphasis.

Stacy smiled tightly. "Totally. Women are the worst."

In her head, though, Stacy was doing quick math. Jeremy had rank, a decent paycheck, and despite his emotional instability, he could *technically* offer her Tricare if she locked him down. Was it ideal? Absolutely not. But Stacy didn't grow up in a Hallmark movie.

Unfortunately, Jeremy spent half the night yelling about his ex and the other half passed out, face-first on his pillow. Stacy decided not even health insurance was worth that level of toxicity.

## Room 109: Lucas – The Sweetheart

And then, there was Lucas. Sweet, naive, wears-his-heart-on-his-sleeve Lucas. Stacy didn't mean to wander into Lucas's life. It just… happened. He invited her in with a smile and offered her water before she even sat down.

"You okay?" Lucas asked, eyes kind and sincere.

No one had asked Stacy that in a long time. She blinked. "Yeah. I'm fine."

Lucas spent the evening showing her pictures of his family, talking about his plans for the future, and playing guitar—*actual guitar,* not just strumming aimlessly. By the end of the night, Stacy felt something weird stirring in her chest. Guilt.

Lucas deserved someone who'd bake him cookies and write letters while he was deployed. Not someone like her, calculating which sailor would get her name on a DEERS form the fastest.

The next morning, Lucas hugged her before she left. Hugged. Who does that?

And what did Stacy do? She turned around, walked straight next door, and hopped into someone else's bed.

Because Stacy's life didn't have room for sweet endings or kind-hearted guys like Lucas. She had a mission, damn it, and no room for distractions.

**The Truth About Stacy**

Here's the thing about barracks bunnies like Stacy: it's easy to judge them. It's easy to snicker and say, "There she goes again," or roll your eyes when her name gets mentioned. But at the end of the day,

Stacy's not some heartless villain. She's just a girl trying to survive in a world that's been hard on her.

She grew up watching her mom fight over unpaid bills. She knows what it's like to sit in a free clinic waiting room, clutching her stomach in pain because she couldn't afford real care. And if she has to hop from room to room, spinning lies and breaking hearts, to make sure she never ends up like that again—then so be it.

You don't have to like Stacy. You don't even have to understand her. But don't pretend her story isn't real, because I guarantee you there's a Stacy on every base, hopping her way to what she thinks is a better life.

And if you're reading this, thinking, "That sounds like someone I know," you're probably right.

# Cynthia

Cynthia gripped the steering wheel tightly as she pulled up to Pier 12 at Norfolk Naval Base. The USS Bataan loomed in the distance, its massive, imposing structure framed against the gray morning sky. Her husband, Mike, sat beside her, fidgeting with the straps of his sea bag. He looked calm, even excited, but Cynthia's stomach churned with unease.

"You'll call when you can, right?" she asked, her voice a little too tight.

Mike reached over, squeezing her hand. "Of course. You've got this. You always do."

Famous last words.

As soon as he stepped out of the car and disappeared into the chaos of the pier, Cynthia felt it—a strange mix of relief, dread, and loneliness. The drive home was quiet, her kids, fast asleep in the back seat. she'd be fine. She always was.

But Murphy's Law had other plans.

**Day 1: Pretending You're Okay**
The first day of deployment is always the hardest. Cynthia woke up to an empty bed, her hand instinctively reaching for Mike's side. It was cold.

She plastered on a brave face for the kids, making their favorite pancakes and laughing at their silly jokes, but inside, she felt like someone had yanked the rug out from under her.

By noon, her friends had started checking in. "How are you holding up?" they'd text, accompanied by heart emojis.

"Fine," she replied each time, because what else could she say? That she felt like a piece of her was missing? That she couldn't stop thinking about how long 8 months actually was?

No, she'd save that for later—for when she cried in the shower so the kids wouldn't hear.

## Day 3: The Dryer Dies

Cynthia was folding laundry when she heard it: a high-pitched screech that could only mean one thing. The dryer was broken.

She hit the start button again, willing it to work, but it was dead. She stared at the damp clothes in disbelief. "Of course," she muttered.

She texted her dad, hoping for some guidance. His response was quick but less than helpful: *"Try unplugging it and plugging it back in."*

"Thanks, tech support," she grumbled, dragging the clothes outside to hang on a makeshift line. It rained an hour later.

## Day 5: The Car Betrayal

Deployment isn't just a test of emotional endurance; it's a full-on battle with your own home. And your car.

Cynthia's trusty minivan started making a clunking noise on her way to the commissary. By the time she got home, the check engine light was glaring at her like an angry boss.

She called the mechanic, praying it wasn't serious. Spoiler: it was. "Looks like your alternator's shot," the mechanic said. "That'll be $1,200."

"Of course it is," Cynthia muttered, mentally rearranging the budget to figure out how they'd afford groceries that month.

## Day 7: The HVAC Mutiny

Just when Cynthia thought she'd caught a break, the air

conditioning decided to quit during an unseasonably warm spring. The house turned into a sauna almost overnight.

"Mom, it's so hot," her youngest whined, flopping onto the couch like a melodramatic fish.

"I know, sweetie," Cynthia said, wiping sweat from her forehead. "We'll survive."

"Will we, though?" her teenager asked, staring at her like she'd lost her mind.

Cynthia didn't have the energy to argue. Instead, she ordered a fan off Amazon and added "call HVAC repair" to her ever-growing to-do list.

**Day 10: Murphy's Law in Full Force**
If there's one thing every military spouse knows, it's that Murphy's Law isn't a one-and-done deal. It's a relentless series of punches designed to test your patience, your resilience, and your ability to Google "DIY home repair."

By the tenth day, Cynthia was dealing with:

- A broken dryer
- A car in the shop
- A house hotter than Satan's living room
- And a raccoon that had taken up residence in her attic

Her friends sent supportive texts, her kids complained constantly, and Cynthia? She was holding it together with duct tape and sarcasm.

When Mike finally called from the ship, Cynthia felt a wave of relief. "How's everything going?" he asked, his voice cheerful and calm.

"Oh, you know," Cynthia said, trying to sound nonchalant. "The dryer broke, the car's in the shop, the AC is dead, and there's a raccoon in the attic. But other than that, I'm great."

Mike chuckled. "Sounds like Murphy's Law got you good."

Cynthia forced a laugh. "Yeah. He's my new roommate."

"You're amazing," Mike said. "I don't know how you do it."

Cynthia muted the call, stared at the ceiling, and muttered, "Neither do I."

Here's the thing about deployment: it's not just about missing your spouse. It's about battling everything life throws at you while pretending you're fine. It's about crying in the car because the mechanic just handed you a $1,200 bill. It's about fixing a leaky pipe at midnight because there's no one else to do it.

But it's also about resilience. About proving to yourself that you can handle it. And when your spouse finally comes home, looking tan, too thin, and in need of a long rest, you'll smile sweetly and say, "Welcome back, honey. Now fix everything."

# Trinity

Trinity met Jason at a bonfire party when they were both fresh out of high school. He had that cocky military swagger that made her heart race, and when he smiled at her, it was like nothing else in the world mattered. Within months, they were married, moving into base housing, and dreaming about the future. She thought she'd found her forever. But forever doesn't always look the way you expect it to.

The first year wasn't terrible. Jason had a temper, sure, but Trinity chalked it up to stress. He was adjusting to military life, and she wanted to be supportive. They talked about starting a family, bought a puppy—a golden Lab named Max—and built what felt like a real partnership. She ignored the little things, like the way he'd slam the door a little too hard when he was upset or how the beer cans in the trash seemed to multiply overnight.

It wasn't until she got pregnant that the cracks started to show.

One night, Jason came home smelling like whiskey and bad decisions. Trinity, four months along and exhausted, asked him if he could ease up on the drinking. She wasn't trying to start a fight; she just wanted him to care as much as she did about the baby.

"Don't fucking tell me what to do," he snapped, his words slurred but his anger sharp.

When she stood her ground, his fist came out of nowhere, slamming into her shoulder and sending her stumbling back. Her hands instinctively went to her belly, shielding the life growing inside her. Jason didn't apologize. He grabbed his keys and left, leaving her in stunned silence.

That was the first time he hit her, but it wouldn't be the last.

Trinity tried to convince herself it was a one-time thing, that the Jason she fell in love with was still in there somewhere. But as the weeks passed, his behavior spiraled. He spent their money faster than she could keep track of it, leaving her to figure out how to pay the bills. She picked up odd jobs—babysitting, cleaning houses, anything to keep the lights on.

One evening, she found an ATM receipt on the counter. Their joint account was empty.

"Where's the rent money?" she asked when he got home, her voice trembling.

Jason shrugged, cracking open a beer. "Don't worry about it. I'll get paid again soon."

Then there was Max, the sweet dog who always wagged his tail no matter how bad things got. Max wasn't safe either. When he knocked over Jason's beer one night, Jason grabbed him by the collar and yanked him so hard the dog yelped.

"Jason, stop!" Trinity yelled, stepping between them.

Jason shoved her aside like she was nothing. "He's my dog. I'll do what I want."

And then came the final blow—the discovery that Jason was cheating. Trinity found out when a woman messaged her on Facebook. The message was short and gut-wrenching: *"I didn't know he was married. I'm so sorry."*

Trinity confronted him that night, holding her phone up like evidence in a courtroom. "What the hell is this?"

Jason didn't even try to deny it. "Maybe if you weren't such a nag, I wouldn't have to go looking elsewhere."

Her anger turned into numbness, a defense mechanism against the constant barrage of pain. She started planning her escape in secret.

The final straw came late one night when Jason came home drunk again. Trinity, seven months pregnant and exhausted, asked him to help with dinner. She barely got the words out before he exploded.

"You're useless," he snarled, lunging at her. His fist connected with her side, and she stumbled into the counter.

That was it. The next morning, while Jason was passed out on the couch, Trinity packed a bag. She grabbed Max, some baby clothes, and enough money to get her out of there. She didn't tell him where she was going. She just left.

She drove to a friend's house three hours away, her hands shaking the entire time. When Jason woke up to an empty house, she was already filing for a restraining order.

It wasn't easy, starting over while pregnant and traumatized, but Trinity found her strength. She got a job, rented a small apartment, and started rebuilding her life.

Jason, on the other hand, got what was coming to him. His command didn't take kindly to his antics, and he found himself facing consequences he couldn't drink his way out of.

Trinity didn't just survive Jason—she escaped him. And while her story might make you angry or sad, it's also a reminder that no matter how bad it gets, there's always a way out.

And as for Jason? Let's just say karma has a way of catching up to men like him.

# Gemma

When Gemma met Quinton in high school, it was like a Nicholas Sparks movie. Or at least, that's how she told it. "We locked eyes across the cafeteria, and I knew he was the one," she'd say, a dreamy look on her face. But let's be real—if Nicholas Sparks were writing this, he'd need to add a disclaimer: *Not suitable for young couples who think love conquers all.* Because Gemma and Quinton? Their love story was more of a cautionary tale than a fairy tale.

They got married straight out of high school, running away from their respective families. Quinton's family was chaos incarnate—think Jerry Springer with extra yelling—while Gemma's was quieter but just as dysfunctional in its own way. They thought getting married would be their great escape, their happily ever after. Spoiler alert: it wasn't.

They packed up their dreams and moved to Jacksonville, Florida. Gemma worked three jobs—yes, three—while Quinton started his Navy career. At first, it was fine. Well, as fine as living in a shoebox apartment with a roommate who stole your food and left socks in the sink could be. But then, the drinking started.

Now, Quinton wasn't always a monster. In the beginning, he was just your run-of-the-mill sailor who thought "hydration" meant another round of Bud Light. But alcohol has a way of revealing the cracks, and boy, did it.

The first time he hit her was the night before a deployment. Gemma, ever the optimist, suggested they spend some quality time together. And by "quality time," she meant sex. Afterward, when she tried to cuddle, Quinton snapped. Literally. He slapped her, threw his steel-toe boot at her face, and broke her nose. Let me repeat that: *he broke her nose with a boot.* And then had the audacity to blame her for not letting him sleep.

Gemma spent that night on the bathroom floor, blood dripping from her face, while Quinton snored in their bed like nothing happened. His friend—*the roommate*—was in the next room and didn't lift a finger. Not even a "Hey, you okay?" Nope. Just crickets.

When Quinton deployed, Gemma adopted a dog—a black lab named Scout—because at least dogs don't throw boots. Scout became her shadow, following her everywhere. One morning, Gemma woke up to a squirrel in the house (thanks to her party-girl roommate leaving the door open). Scout, being the overzealous athlete he was, chased it outside. Gemma, in her fuzzy socks and pajamas, ended up chasing Scout through the snow for an hour. Picture it: a tiny woman, yelling at a dog, slipping on ice, and cursing the universe. That was Gemma's life.

Amid all this chaos, Gemma discovered she was pregnant. Finally, a glimmer of hope. But hope, it seemed, wasn't in the cards. The pregnancy ended in a miscarriage—her third loss. Alone and heartbroken, Gemma emailed Quinton. His response? A couple of lines, barely acknowledging her pain.

By then, Gemma had had enough of the roommate and the apartment. She moved in with her best friend while her husband was underway, and for the first time in ages, she felt free. They had a blast—beach days, late-night talks, even a few questionable decisions. But just as Gemma started to feel normal, Quinton sent her an email accusing her of cheating, lying, and who knows what else. Meanwhile, he was draining their bank account overseas, buying who-knows-what.

The accusations stung, but Gemma fired back. Her response was basically a novel of truths he didn't want to hear: about his drinking, his abuse, and the time he broke her nose. Quinton's reply? "I want a divorce." Classy, right?

When Quinton finally came home, he acted like nothing happened. And Gemma, despite her better judgment, played along. But one night, she confronted him. "What the fuck happened?" she asked. Quinton's response? "What happens on deployment stays on deployment." Gemma didn't buy it, but she wasn't exactly innocent either. In a moment of weakness, she admitted she'd made a mistake too. To her surprise, he didn't care. They both knew they'd messed up.

Things escalated again when Gemma got pregnant for the fourth time. This one stuck, but the abuse didn't stop. Quinton called her fat, lazy, and worse, even as she juggled two jobs and pregnancy. The final straw came when he pushed her down the stairs. Miraculously, both she and the baby were okay, but Gemma knew she couldn't keep living like this.

One night, Quinton grabbed her by the throat and choked her in front of their five-month-old son, Cody. That was it. Gemma grabbed a high chair tray and smashed it into his face. It was the only time she ever hit him, and it was enough. Quinton laughed, a sinister, chilling sound, and taunted her: "Now I can get full custody because you left a mark."

Gemma cried, not because she felt guilty, but because she knew he was right. She hadn't documented his abuse—no photos, no reports, nothing. She'd been too focused on surviving to think about evidence.

Quinton went to the ER that night, spinning a story that kept Gemma out of trouble. When they got home, he broke down, crying and apologizing. He promised to change, and for the first time, Gemma believed him. She gave him an ultimatum: get help or lose them both.

Quinton chose help. He went to AA, anger management, and therapy. Meanwhile, Gemma took Cody and went to Maine to stay with her family, telling them it was just a break while Quinton trained. For months, they worked on themselves separately. Quinton sent proof of his progress, and eventually, Gemma came home.

Things were good. No, they were great. Until Gemma found out Quinton had slept with his coworker during their separation. She didn't yell or cry. Instead, she confronted them calmly, laying out her pain like a lawyer presenting evidence. Both Quinton and the women apologized, but the betrayal cut deep.

Gemma moved into the guest room, taking months to process everything. When she was ready, she and Quinton had a marathon conversation—12 hours of raw, honest talk about their past, their pain, and their future. They decided to rebuild, not for Cody, but for themselves.

And you know what? They did it. They grew up, faced their demons, and came out stronger. Today, Gemma and Quinton are the couple people root for again. Not because they're perfect, but because they're real. They've been through hell and back, and somehow, they made it.

Some might say Gemma should've left. But she sees it differently. She sees a boy who didn't know how to love and a man who worked to learn. And now? Now, they're living proof that love isn't perfect, it's messy, it's painful, but sometimes, it's worth fighting for.

# Emily

On the surface, Emily was a devoted military wife—a little too devoted, if you ask me. She was the kind of spouse who posted inspirational quotes about sacrifice and "holding it down while my man fights for our country." Her Facebook was a shrine to her husband, complete with grainy selfies captioned *"I miss you, baby #deploymentlife #armystrong."*

But behind that glittering wall of social media devotion was a woman weaving a web of lies so tangled it could've trapped a Navy SEAL.

Her husband, let's call him Mark, deployed overseas, ready to serve his country. A few weeks later, Emily dropped the bomb: "I'm pregnant."

Now, Mark was thrilled. Overjoyed, even. Maybe a little confused because, well, *timing*, but hey—military couples make long-distance work, right? Love conquers all. Or at least, that's what he told himself as Emily sent him proof.

Oh, and she didn't skimp on the proof, either. Emily delivered:

- Photos of positive pregnancy tests? Check.
- Ultrasound photos that looked straight out of a doctor's office? Check.
- Growing baby bump pics, complete with her hand lovingly cradling her belly? *Double* check.

Emily had the receipts, and Mark believed every single one. Why wouldn't he? His wife was back home, building a life for the baby boy they were about to have. He started picking out names. He cried to his buddies at night, telling them how he couldn't wait to hold his son. It was the one thing getting him through deployment.

And then, disaster struck.

Mark got a Red Cross call. If you don't know, a Red Cross call is never good news. It's the military's "drop everything and go home" system. And the message was devastating: Emily had been attacked. She'd lost the baby.

Now, picture Mark, sitting in the middle of a combat zone, processing those words. He was crushed. His unborn son was gone. His wife had been brutalized. The Red Cross arranged for him to come home immediately.

He spent the entire flight back drowning in grief, his face buried in his hands, tears streaming down his cheeks as passengers pretended not to notice the soldier quietly breaking apart in seat 27B.

But when he landed? Oh, honey, *the truth* was waiting for him at the gate like an unpaid tab.

Mark wasn't greeted by a somber escort or even Emily's tear-streaked face. Nope. Instead, he was met by military officials ready to ask him some very uncomfortable questions. Turns out, the Red Cross report? Fake. The attack? Fake. The miscarriage? FAKE. The *entire pregnancy*? You guessed it—fake.

Emily had cooked up the most elaborate lie anyone on base had ever heard. She faked the test, faked the ultrasounds (courtesy of Google Images, no doubt), and even stuffed her shirts to make her belly look "pregnant." But Emily didn't stop there—oh no. She threw herself fully into the role, waddling around Walmart like she was nine months along and posting tearful statuses like, *"Feeling little kicks today #grateful."*

And the attack? That was the pièce de résistance of her insanity. She fabricated a brutal assault, complete with dramatic phone calls to friends saying, "I just don't know if I'll ever recover." Meanwhile, Mark was still on the other side of the world, clutching his heart in anguish for a woman who deserved an Academy Award, not sympathy.

When the truth finally hit him—when officials explained what *really* happened—Mark nearly broke down right there. He was still processing the "loss" of a son who never existed. The betrayal? Unimaginable.

And Emily? Well, Emily didn't have a whole lot to say when it all unraveled. She sat in her living room, shrugging like a kid who got caught sneaking cookies before dinner.

"I just wanted him to come home," she reportedly said, as if *that* made her web of lies any better.

Now, I know what you're thinking: "How does someone pull this off?" Honestly? I have no idea. The lengths some people go to for attention, sympathy, or control are both impressive and terrifying.

And poor Mark—he was just a guy trying to survive deployment, dreaming about holding his imaginary son, only to come home and get blindsided by the plot twist of the decade.

So, let this be a cautionary tale: Sometimes the people you trust the most are the ones hiding the craziest secrets. And if you ever get a Red Cross call during deployment? Maybe ask for a second opinion.

As for Emily? Well, I heard she quietly disappeared off base after that. Probably to start a new chapter of her life—preferably far, far away from the nearest military installation.

And if you're out there, Emily, sipping your pumpkin spice latte and pretending none of this happened, just know… your story made it into a book. *Congratulations.*

# Brandy

Let's take a leisurely stroll down base housing lane and meet the one and only Brandy—because *every* base has a Brandy. You might not know her personally, but you've seen her. She's the one peeking through her curtains when you pull into the driveway, taking notes like she's an unpaid private investigator.

Brandy's husband is an E6 in the Navy. A hardworking man—emphasis on *working*. The poor guy holds down three jobs because someone has to fund Brandy's full-time "lifestyle." You know, the one where she buys useless home décor that never actually gets hung up, random Amazon orders that no one ever sees again, and about 12 varieties of face creams she never uses because she's too busy sleeping through the day.

Now, let's talk about Brandy's hobbies. Wait. Scratch that. Brandy doesn't have hobbies. Unless, of course, you count being nosy as one. She's the self-appointed drama coordinator for the entire block. If there's a rumor to be spread, Brandy's already at your doorstep with "concerned" eyebrows and a fake sympathetic nod.

"Did you hear about Jessica? Her husband's car was parked at the barracks again. You didn't hear it from me, though."

Oh, Brandy. We *always* hear it from you.

Brandy's mornings are simple:

1. Wake up at 10 AM.
2. Yell at one of her four kids to make her coffee.

3. Stand in the driveway in pajama pants with her arms crossed, *watching*. Watching who comes and goes, what's getting delivered, and who might be due for a good gossip session.

Her husband, meanwhile, is probably halfway through his second shift at the gas station or side gigging as a DoorDash driver because someone has to keep the lights on.

Now, you might be wondering, "What about her kids?" Oh, Brandy loves her kids—she just prefers not to parent them. "They're independent," she'll say proudly while her toddler attempts to ride the neighbor's dog like a pony and her 12-year-old demolishes a box of cereal for dinner. The kids have a routine, though: wake up, feed themselves, and stay out of Brandy's hair until she's good and ready to yell at them for "being too loud."

Brandy, bless her heart, also refuses to work. "I can't trust anyone to watch my kids," she'll say, with a dramatic sigh as she plops onto her sofa. Ma'am, you've got four kids who've been raising themselves since they could crawl—they don't need a babysitter; they need *snacks*.

Let's not forget Brandy's favorite pastime: meddling. She's always got one foot jammed in someone else's life. Whether she's pretending to offer advice or fishing for information, Brandy will insert herself like she's been hired to solve *everyone's* problems.

"I'm just trying to help!" she'll say, innocently, right after she's told the entire neighborhood about Jenny's divorce or Ashley's husband sneaking off base with a "friend."

But here's the kicker—Brandy doesn't trust *anyone*. Not one soul. "People are fake," she'll mutter, side-eyeing you like you're plotting against her. This might explain why Brandy doesn't have friends. Sure, she'll text you the second she spots your kid's bike lying on the lawn ("Did you *know* it was out there?"), but don't expect her to invite you in for coffee. She doesn't trust you, and honestly? You don't like her.

You might be tempted to feel bad for Brandy's husband, E6 Superdad, but don't worry—he's too exhausted to notice. Between balancing the Navy, side jobs, and coming home to his kids building a fort out of unopened Amazon boxes, the man is basically a walking shell of himself.

And here's the truth about Brandy: she's exhausting, she's dramatic, and she's *everywhere*. But maybe, just maybe, underneath all that nosiness and laziness, she's just a little bit lonely.

Or maybe she's just terrible. It's a toss-up.

# Green Tea

Ah, the *Dependapotomus*—a creature of legend, whispered about in FRG meetings and commissary checkout lines. If you've ever been within a 50-mile radius of a military base, you've probably encountered one, even if you didn't realize it at the time. They blend in during the day, their camouflage consisting of "Navy Wife: Toughest Job in the Military" hoodies and oversized sunglasses, but don't be fooled. When the Starbucks run is done and the daycare closes, the drama comes out.

A *Dependa* isn't just any military spouse. No, no. She's an *experience*. Picture this: Amber is in the commissary parking lot, her husband's rank prominently displayed on the bumper sticker of her minivan—because how else will people know her social status? She steps out, cradling a designer bag that probably cost more than her husband's entire paycheck, her phone glued to her hand as she FaceTimes her bestie about "those lazy lower enlisted wives" who dare to park in the officer section.

"Oh my god, Becky," she says, dramatically flipping her highlighted hair, "I told the base housing office that I need granite countertops, not this *cheap laminate crap*. Do they not know my husband's an E-6? Like, honestly."

Meanwhile, her three kids are in the backseat, fighting over a Happy Meal toy, one of them covered head-to-toe in Cheeto dust, while the baby shrieks like a banshee. But worry not—she is unbothered. She's got a manicure appointment to make, and little Timmy's tantrum can wait.

**Let's Break Down the Behavior**

1. **The Rank Dropper**:
   the Rank dropper firmly believes her husband's rank is also hers. "My husband is a Chief, so I should get the best

parking spots at the commissary, a front-row seat at command events, and preferential treatment at the clinic." Girl, sit down. Rank doesn't transfer via marriage license.

2. **The Financial Assassin**:
   Oh, the spending habits. *Dependas* are the reason why payday feels like a holiday for military families and a horror movie the next day. New iPhones for the kids? Check. Louis Vuitton bag for herself? Double check. Husband's credit card maxed out by noon? You already know. Meanwhile, poor Sergeant Daniels is eating tuna from a pouch, wondering how they're going to make it to the next payday.

3. **Drama's Best Friend**:
   A *Dependa* doesn't just thrive on gossip—she manufactures it. You think you're safe? Wrong. She's already told the FRG that your husband forgot to salute his CO that one time, and now you're both the hot topic at the next command barbecue. She lives for it, bathes in it, breathes it in like it's oxygen.

4. **The Social Media Warrior**:
   "Being a military wife is the hardest job in the world," she writes, captioning a selfie with a full face of makeup, holding a venti Frappuccino. Her Facebook timeline is a minefield of passive-aggressive memes, motivational quotes about sacrifice (she doesn't work), and poorly lit photos of her husband looking miserable during a change-of-command ceremony.

**An Average Day in the Life**

Let me set the scene: Amber rolls into the base gym, her water bottle plastered with motivational stickers and her gym bag slung over her shoulder. Except she's not here to work out. Oh no. She's here to "network."

"Hey, Brittany," she says, sidling up to a group of actual gym-goers. "Did you hear about Jessica? Her husband got a counseling chit last week. Can you *imagine*?" She doesn't even break a sweat, but by the time she leaves, Jessica's reputation is in tatters, and Amber feels victorious.

Later, she's at the housing office, complaining about her neighbor's dog barking at 10 p.m. "It's a *health hazard*," she insists, while secretly plotting how to get her family bumped to the top of the housing list.

**In Conclusion**
Not every military spouse is a *Dependa*. In fact, most are hardworking, supportive, and doing their best to hold it all together. But the *Dependa*? She's in a league of her own. Equal parts entertaining and exasperating, she's the reason FRG meetings have a reputation, why command wives side-eye each other at events, and why the term "bless your heart" was invented.

So, the next time you're at the commissary and you spot someone in a rhinestone "Proud Military Wife" hoodie, remember: you're in the presence of greatness—or, at the very least, a damn good story.

# Lacey

Military relationships. They're a unique brand of chaos, aren't they? You think you're signing up for love, shared Netflix accounts, and maybe the occasional argument over who left the milk out. But then—surprise! You find yourself navigating rank structures, acronyms, and unsolicited lectures about why you can't call a drill sergeant, well…a drill sergeant. Meet Lacey, the queen of patience—at least on most days.

Lacey's boyfriend, Preston, is a Marine. And not just any Marine—Preston would have you believe he's the Marine. Think Captain America meets a motivational speaker who also moonlights as a walking recruitment poster. He's loud, proud, and—if you ask Lacey—about two steps away from requesting people salute him at the dinner table.

When they first started dating, it was kind of endearing. Lacey liked his confidence, his passion for his work, and, okay, maybe the uniform didn't hurt. But now, a year in, it's starting to feel less like love and more like being trapped in an endless episode of *Military Men Say the Darndest Things.*

Take last weekend, for example. Lacey had planned a casual dinner with her friends, hoping Preston would finally get to know her world a little better. Instead, he turned the evening into a TED Talk titled "How I Dominated My Role as the Marine Corps' Gift to Earth."

"You know, as an officer in the Corps," Preston began, swirling his drink like he was at a gala instead of a pizza joint, "it's my job to inspire the enlisted. Just the other day, I had to really lay into one of my guys because he didn't salute properly."

Lacey cringed. "Oh, wow, that sounds… intense," she managed, glancing at her friends, who were doing their best to look polite while internally screaming for help.

The thing is, Preston hadn't deployed. Not once. He lived on base near the beach, worked a cushy desk job, and spent his evenings curating the perfect Instagram posts about his "service." Yet he spoke like he was fresh from storming Normandy.

Then there was the "War-Dog" incident. Lacey was still trying to recover from the sheer secondhand embarrassment of it all. They were at a barbecue with some of Preston's colleagues when he casually asked someone to call him a War-Dog. A War. Dog. Lacey nearly choked on her soda.

It wasn't just the cringe-worthy nicknames, though. Preston's ego bled into everything. Grocery shopping turned into a mini boot camp when Lacey made the grave error of calling someone a drill sergeant.

"If you want to be an officer's wife," Preston snapped, "you need to understand the proper terms. That's not a drill sergeant—it's a drill instructor."

Lacey blinked, holding a bag of frozen peas like a grenade she wanted to lob at his head.

"Cool. And if you want to be my husband, you might want to chill."

She wasn't sure how much longer she could keep this up. Every conversation circled back to the Marines. Every story was a dramatic retelling of how Preston saved the day, even if it was just organizing some paperwork. Her friends avoided hanging out with them because they couldn't handle Preston's self-importance.

And his family? Oh, they ate it up. Lacey once sat through two hours of him regaling his parents with tales of his "heroic" day-to-day life, and not once did they ask her how she was doing. By the end of the night, she felt like a piece of furniture—present but completely invisible.

What really got her, though, was the lack of balance. Lacey wasn't asking Preston to ignore his work or stop being proud of what he did. But did every conversation have to turn into a monologue about the Corps? Did he have to mansplain every little thing, as if she hadn't been living in the same world as him for the past year?

One night, Lacey had enough. "Preston," she said, after enduring yet another long-winded story about how he corrected some poor soul on base, "do you even know what I do for work?"

Preston blinked. "Of course I do. You, uh… do something with computers, right?"

"I'm a graphic designer."

"Right. That's what I said."

Lacey stared at him. "No, it's not. And for the record, I don't expect you to know every detail of my job, but maybe we could talk about something that's not the Marines for once? Like, I don't know, literally anything else?"

Preston looked genuinely confused, as if the concept of non-Marine-related conversation was a foreign language. "But I thought you liked hearing about my work?"

"I did. At first. But now, it's all you talk about, and it's…a lot. Can we just be us? Without the titles and the ranks and the constant Marine Corps infomercials?"

To Preston's credit, he seemed to take her words to heart—at least for a little while. But Lacey knew she had a decision to make. The ick was growing, and if she didn't address it, she'd end up resenting him forever.

The real question wasn't whether she loved Preston. It was whether she could love him without losing herself in the process.

And as much as she hoped he'd tone it down, part of her knew she couldn't spend the rest of her life competing with the Marines for his attention.

But hey, at least she'd always have the "War-Dog" story to laugh about.

# Brooke

Japan—the land of sushi, cherry blossoms, and Nintendo. For Brooke and Joseph, the high-rise military apartments that scrape the sky are "home sweet home."

Picture it: Brooke, our heroine (or anti-heroine, depending on your perspective), comes through the door of their modest apartment in Yokosuka, Dependent ID still dangling from her neck. She's just finished a grueling shift at the local movie theater, popping popcorn and reminding rowdy teenagers to keep their phones off during the latest Marvel blockbuster. She tosses her bag on the counter, kicks off her shoes—not quite into the designated shoe rack, mind you—and flops onto the couch with a deep sigh.

Enter Joseph. The handsome overworked husband. He's just finished another 12-hour shift onboard the USS Shit Bucket (okay, the USS Bataan). His uniform is still crisp despite the humidity of Japan's summers, and he's balancing a bag of groceries in one hand and his lunchbox in the other. Oh, and don't forget the heavy-duty, cat-litter-scented trash bag dangling from his wrist—because someone has to deal with Noodle's unholy bathroom habits.

"Hey," Joseph says, his voice as calm and warm as ever. "How was your day?"

Brooke doesn't even look up from her book. "Long," she replies, flipping a page with the theatrical energy of someone carrying the weight of the world. "I stood for, like, eight hours."

Joseph nods, unfazed, as he begins unloading the groceries. Eggs, milk, some local Japanese snacks Brooke loves but never remembers to buy. He quickly moves on to the litter box—a monstrosity in the corner of the kitchen. The villain's minion? Noodle. A rotund, unbothered tabby currently stretched across the dining table like a furry Roman emperor.

"Hey, buddy," Joseph mutters as he scoops out what can only be described as toxic waste. "You've been busy, huh?"

Noodle doesn't respond. He's too busy judging Joseph for not petting him first. Because, of course, in Noodle's world, humans are there for his convenience, not the other way around.

As Joseph sweeps, mops, and tosses in a load of laundry, Brooke remains planted on the couch, her book now resting on the armrest as she doom-scrolls through her phone. "What are we doing for dinner?" she calls out lazily.

"I'll cook something," Joseph replies, trying not to sound exasperated. Because, you see, Joseph has a secret superpower: patience. And boy, does he need it.

Now, let's pause for a moment, dear reader. Because I have something to say.

Look, I get it. Work is exhausting. No one's denying that. But let me be clear: Brooke has no kids. No additional mouths to feed, no tantrums to mediate. Just a husband who works longer hours than she does and a cat whose primary contribution to society is shedding fur on clean laundry. Housework? It should be split. Fairly. If one partner is working their tail off, the other has to pick up some slack.

It's teamwork, not "he works, she rests." But I guess some people just don't get the memo. Anyway, back to the story.

After dinner, a simple but delicious stir-fry courtesy of Chef Joseph, he settles into the living room with his gaming headset. This is his time to unwind, chatting with his friends back home and blowing off steam in the virtual world of "Call of Duty."

Brooke, meanwhile, is back to her book, curled up on the couch with a glass of wine. You'd think peace had finally descended on the household. But no.

"Do you have to play those games every night?" Brooke asks suddenly, not looking up from her book.

Joseph hesitates, the loading screen reflecting in his glasses. "I'm just playing for an hour or two. It helps me relax."

"Well, it's loud," she says, even though she's reading a Kindle with noise-canceling earbuds in.

Now, let's just address the elephant in the room—or in this case, the living room. Brooke, like many, is quick to criticize Joseph's gaming hobby. But here's the kicker: her reading takes up far more time than his gaming. Hours spent curled up in a book, absorbed in fictional worlds, while Joseph's gaming sessions max out at maybe two hours on a busy day. It's a double standard as old as time. Before you roll your eyes at someone's hobby, maybe take a good, long look in the mirror. Because if anyone's absent, it's not Joseph.

Joseph doesn't argue. He adjusts the volume and leans back, trying to enjoy his hard-earned downtime. Meanwhile, Noodle waddles over, climbing onto Brooke's lap and promptly digging his claws into her thigh.

"Seriously, Noodle?" she yelps, pushing him off.

Noodle, the king of the apartment, lands gracefully on the floor and flicks his tail in annoyance. He stomps over to Joseph instead, plopping down at his feet and looking up expectantly.

"What's up, bud?" Joseph asks, pausing his game to give Noodle some head scratches.

Brooke rolls her eyes. "He's just using you to get treats."

"Yeah, well," Joseph says with a shrug, tossing Noodle a little snack from the container on the coffee table, "at least he appreciates me."

The jab is subtle, but it lands. Brooke looks up, guilt flashing across her face for the briefest of moments. "I appreciate you," she mutters, though it sounds more like a question than a statement.

Joseph doesn't respond. He's already back in his game, Noodle now perched on his lap like a furry good-luck charm.

The evening ends as it always does: Joseph logging off, Brooke finishing her book, and Noodle claiming the best spot on the bed while the humans argue over whose turn it is to move him.

And so, another day in the life of Brooke, Joseph, and Noodle comes to a close. But as the lights go out and the apartment falls silent, you can't help but wonder: how long can one person carry the weight of the household before they break? Or, perhaps more importantly, when will Brooke realize that sometimes love means more than just saying "I appreciate you"? It means showing it—preferably by scooping the damn litter box once in a while.

# Alyssa

As anyone who's ever been married can tell you, real life isn't a Hallmark movie. It's a chaotic mess of bad decisions, broken trust, and sometimes, one *really* shady mother-in-law. This? This is one of those stories.

Noah joined the Navy right after graduating in September 2018. He was the proud kid in a fresh uniform, ready to take on the world. Boot camp? Check. Stationed in sunny San Diego? Double check. Life was good. Alyssa stayed behind, but after a year of long-distance calls and tearful goodbyes, they tied the knot. She was supposed to join him overseas eventually, but life, being the relentless plot-twister it is, had other plans.

Noah got orders to Sasebo, Japan, and Alyssa decided to stay behind, claiming she wanted to join the Navy herself. "Fine," Noah thought, "it's temporary." He stayed loyal during his year in Japan, no sketchy situations, no late-night regrets. Meanwhile, Alyssa stayed in the States, and her family faced a devastating tragedy: a drunk driver killed her dad and younger sister in a horrific head-on collision. Her mom and other sister survived but were left shattered.

Being the good husband he was, Noah took emergency leave and flew home to be there for Alyssa and her family. He stepped into the father figure role, doing everything he could to help them rebuild. But even then, something felt... off. There were whispers about Alyssa's mom using the life insurance money for extravagant trips and luxuries. Noah brushed it off, because who wants to believe their in-laws are shady? Spoiler: they were.

Fast forward to his next set of orders. Noah got stationed in Norfolk, Virginia, and Alyssa followed, finally living together as a couple. Noah did everything to make the transition smooth, he got her a car, found a cute duplex, and even helped her mom and sister move into the other side of the duplex. Everything seemed fine. That is until Noah's best friend and roommate, burst into the room one night, drunk.

"She groped me!" Noah's best friend yelled. Alyssa's mom, yes, *the mom*, had made a move on him, trying to kiss him and getting way too handsy. When confronted, she shrugged it off, delivering some bizarre monologue about "open relationships" and how she just "takes what she wants."

Disgusted? Same.

Soon after, Noah went on deployment. Communication was spotty at best, with restricted internet access, and no time for long calls, you know the drill. But even in the brief moments they spoke, red flags started popping up like weeds in a garden. Alyssa casually mentioned a new "best friend", gushing about how *amazing* he was.

Noah's Spidey senses were tingling. And when Alyssa dropped this gem during one call "Andrew says he likes his girlfriends with long hair so he can pull it while they fuck", Noah was done. Who even *says* that? Oh, and right after that, she asked for an open marriage. Because of course, she did.

Noah laid down the law: because it wasn't the first time she had asked him this.

"Absolutely not. Ask me that again, and we're done," he warned.

Weeks later, Noah got an email. Alyssa wanted a "break" to "find herself." Translation? She wanted to find Andrew in her bed.

When Noah returned from deployment, he was met with radio silence. Alyssa didn't even bother to pick him up herself. Instead, her mom showed up at a McDonald's, hugged him, and took him home. The house felt... wrong. The warmth it once had was gone, replaced by an icy tension Noah couldn't ignore.

That night, he stumbled across a journal on the bed. Curiosity got the better of him, and what he found inside shattered him. It was a diary, Alyssa's diary, detailing her affair with Andrew. Every entry was worse than the last. They'd been passing the journal back and forth on their ship, writing love letters, planning secret meetups, and yes, documenting their sex life in excruciating detail.

One entry stood out: Alyssa had crossed out Noah's last name and replaced it with Andrew's. Oh, and she was pregnant. The military instruction for breastfeeding in uniform, casually tucked into the journal, confirmed it.

Noah sat on the floor, rage and heartbreak swallowing him whole. When Alyssa came home, he didn't yell. He didn't cry at first. He simply sat on the couch, journal in hand, and read every single word aloud. By the end, tears streamed down his face, but his voice remained steady.

"Get the fuck out of my house," he said. "You're going to make a great mom. Just not here."

Cue Alyssa's mom storming in, yelling at Noah for "yelling at her daughter." Wrong move. Noah let her have it, calling out her shady behavior, her lavish vacations, and the way she sexually harassed his friends. The cops were called, but Noah kept his cool, calmly explaining the situation when they arrived.

The officers escorted him back inside to grab his things, and he left to stay with a friend. When he returned the next day, Alyssa and her family were gone. They'd stripped the place bare, leaving behind one thing: her wedding ring on the counter.

Noah didn't cry. Instead, he went camping. He took that ring, loaded it into his shotgun, and shot it into oblivion.

Here's the thing: no amount of love, loyalty, or effort can fix a relationship built on a shaky foundation. Noah gave everything to his marriage, but Alyssa, and her circus of a family, proved they weren't worth the fight.

So, to Noah? Good riddance, my dude. You dodged not just a bullet, but an entire dumpster fire. And to Alyssa and Andrew? Well, karma's a patient beast.

# Jenna

Alright, dear reader—it's time for a little confession. You've flipped through the drama, the chaos, the tears, and the tea, and now you're probably wondering, "Who is this sassy narrator anyway? Who is this person spilling all the gossip and throwing shade like it's her part-time job?"

Well... hi. It's me. I'm in here. My story? Oh, it's in these pages. Remember that chapter about the base housing being a moldy, crusty nightmare? The one where you thought, "Surely this is exaggerated for entertainment value?" Yeah... no. That was me. Your girl lived in a place so gross it could have qualified as an entry on a horror movie set. Honestly, at one point I half-expected to find a family of raccoons paying rent in my walls. But hey, character building, right?

And since you've been along for this wild ride, I figured I'd share a little personal tea—because who doesn't love a good love story with a side of "Wait, really?"

Picture this: 6th grade. Middle school. 2005. I was rocking frizzy hair that had a mind of its own (humidity was not my friend), and there he was—my future husband. Frosted tips, a wardrobe consisting entirely of basketball shorts and skate shoes, and the personality of that kid who definitely thought he was funnier than he was. And what did he do? He bulled me.

Fast forward to high school, and somewhere between hallway run-ins and shared classes, we became friends—like, actual friends.

The kind who swapped playlists and talked about life during lunch breaks. Then, as fate (and teenage hormones) would have it, we started dating. Who knew the guy who literally threw me in the garbage can on the first day of high school would be the one holding my hand at prom? (yes, he did that)

And because we love a good plot twist, we got married straight out of high school. Yep. Full send. No hesitations, just two teenagers with hearts full of dreams (and heads full of questionable decisions). And what did we do? Packed up our lives and moved 3,000 miles away to Virginia. Nothing screams "romantic adventure" like figuring out how to adult in a new state with no money, no friends, and a GPS that constantly lied to us.

And let me tell you... base housing? Yeah, that was part of the "charm." Moldy walls, leaky ceilings, and neighbors who argued loud enough to be featured on reality TV. We stuck it out through the chaos—deployments, moves, that one time I found a cockroach the size of a Twinkie in the kitchen... ah, the memories!

But through it all—the drama, the tears, the mildew-covered walls—we made it work. He's still the guy who drives me nuts, makes me laugh, and occasionally reminds me of that one time he had frosted tips (yes, I have photos. No, you can't see them).

So yeah... my story is in here. It's messy. It's hilarious. It's real. And if you take nothing else from this book, let it be this: life is wild, love is weird, and sometimes the boy who literally threw you in a trash can ends up being the man you share a mortgage and Netflix account with.

# Chamomile Tea

Well, we've reached the end, haven't we? The last sip, the dregs of the pot, the point where I leave you sitting there, staring at this book like it just set your favorite soap opera on fire and walked out the door with your popcorn. But don't worry, dear reader, I'm not leaving you empty-handed. I'll leave you with this: every sip of tea we've shared, every story, every jaw-dropping revelation, it's just the beginning.

You see, what I've served you in these pages is but a single teapot in an endless collection. There are so many more stories to tell. So many more wives with secrets, so many more "dependas" with drama, and yes, so many more military husbands who think they're untouchable (spoiler: they're not).

That's right. If you thought this book was something, you haven't even begun to imagine the *shitstorm* of chaos that swirls around the men in uniform. Oh, you think the wives are bad? Sweetheart, let me introduce you to *deployments gone wrong, barracks escapades,* and *husbands who think "away on orders" is code for "live like you're on spring break."*

But here's the thing: I can't tell all the stories in one sitting. This tea kettle needs a break before it whistles itself into oblivion. The stories I've shared with you are just the tip of the iceberg. I have entire pots of piping hot tea waiting to be brewed, and trust me, it's so scandalous, so ridiculous, you'll wonder how these people still manage to function as adults.

And while we're on the subject of functioning adults, let's not pretend this is a one-sided phenomenon. For every "dependa" you've gasped at, there's a husband out there doing his own brand of unhinged. Men who burn through paychecks faster than they can say "Hooyah." Men who ghost their wives during deployment only to reappear with suspicious tan lines and *souvenirs they definitely didn't get from the base exchange.* Men who, well, you'll just have to wait for that one, won't you?

Here's what I'll leave you with: The world of military life is messy, chaotic, and absurd. It's full of love, betrayal, drama, and, let's be honest, enough material to keep me writing until the end of time. And if you're sitting there thinking, *I can't believe this stuff is real,* let me assure you, it is. Every story, every wild turn of events, it's all been spilled from real cups of tea. The names have been changed, but the chaos? Oh, that's 100% authentic.

So, pour yourself another cup, settle in, and start praying for a sequel. Because if you thought *this* was wild, wait until you see what happens when we flip the script and spill the tea about the men.

Until next time, my friend, keep your cups ready. Trust me, the tea is far from finished.

Want your story featured in the next book? Whether you're a military spouse with some jaw-dropping drama or a service member with deployment chaos and wild shenanigans to share—I want to hear it! Send me a message on Instagram **@S.A.L.O.M.W.** and you just might see your story in the next installment. Don't worry, names will be changed to protect the *guilty*—I mean, innocent.

Made in the USA
Middletown, DE
31 March 2025